The Best-Kept Secret **Of The Car Insurance Industry.**

VISIT US

American Insurance Advocate Group
www.AmericanInsuranceAdvocateGroup.com

Contents

What You

Need to Know about Diminished Value?

Diminished Value or commonly known as DV refer to the terms that are used in describing the economic loss of the value of the property as the result of being damaged. DV or Diminished Value is always associated with the vehicles that were damaged, but this is also applicable to some properties like real estate, jewelry and even artwork.

Diminished Value Defined

Diminished Value or DV is defined as the portion of the pre-Loss Value of the damaged vehicle that was not restored through the process of repair.

Even if the vehicle has been properly repaired, this will not have the similar value on the resale market compared to the car that has the same model as well as year, which hasn't been into an accident. As results, the diminished value is actually the difference between the car's market value that hasn't been damaged as well as the amount for which the car is sold. Numerous insurance companies provide policies which allow car owners to compensate for this depreciation in value. However, this is only possible if it was the fault of someone else in the accident, yet some states do allow you to claim DV against your own policy in some instances or even in the case of an accident where it is the at fault party when the state allow it such as Georgia, Washington, Kansas or even North Carolina.

If persons with car insurance get into accidents, the insurance company will basically pay off the claim, which car owners can use for necessary fixes or repairs. Even though the car was repaired properly and it runs smoothly or looks the same as brand new cars, there's often an attached stigma to the car in potential buyers' eyes. This is known as the diminished value, the amount of the car's value that was lost after this has been involved into an accident.

The main reason that the diminished value exists is that some buyers of used cars always hesitate at buying a car that was involved into an accident as much as 80% of buyers. Even though repairs are effective, the thing is that the car was damaged. Since this is the situation, those who are selling

cars that have been into accidents will have no choice but to offer their car at a particular discount.

Fortunately for several car owners, there are some ways to recover diminished value. Some particular insurance policies allow protection against loss of car's value that was involved in accidents. Aside from payment for necessary repairs, such policies will also assist offset value that was loss, which can provide policy holders that were not fault during the accident.

There are basically three basic kinds of Diminished Value and these are as follows:

1. Immediate Diminished Value

This is the difference in resale value of the car immediately before there were damages occurred as well as immediately after the damage occurred. Majority of jurisdictions make use of this standard. This will serve as the damage's primary measure when courts were employed to search for reimbursement for the damages from the negligent party. Since courts are not usually the selected venue for property damage's recovery, this type of diminished value is not always employed to resolve the damages and get claims on the property damage.

2. Inherent Diminished Value

This type of DV assumes maximum repair quality that was achieved and defined as the amount in which the repaired vehicle's resale value was reduced just because of its involvement into an accident. This diminished value is considered as the most recognized as well as accepted form by many people. This is also a basis upon any supplemental forms of diminished value could be added. Another form is repair related diminished value.

3. Repair Related Diminished Value

This includes any extra amounts through which the subject vehicle's resale value may further reduced due to the lesser optimal repairs.

This might also include anything from the minor cosmetic imperfections to main structural defects.

INSURANCE REFERENCE TERMS

If you're one of those who are new in studying the insurance law, you might be confused by the references especially when it comes to third party and first party claims. You might be also wondering about the persons involved and the second party. Such terms were derived from references to insurance policy that serves as a contract.

There are 2 parties included in an insurance contract. These are the insurance company and the insured. Through practice and custom, the insured is considered as the first party while the second party is the insurance company. However, for some reasons, this is seldom referred in this manner. When it comes to the policy, the stranger is the third party. This is someone who is either the insurer or the insured.

First Party

The first party claim is the one that should be paid to the insured directly. The claim for property damage under the policy of homeowners is a great example of the first party claim. When the insured has suffered property loss, if it is covered by the company, the insurance company needs to pay him. Coverage, which provides some benefits, is typically considered as the first party coverage.

Third Party

The third party claim is the one which involves harm or damage to the third party like someone aside from the one insured. Usually, this is if not often, a liability claim. When and if the claim is settled, the money will be paid to the third party or claimant instead of the insured. A usual sample of the third party claim is the lawsuit against the insured driver that is negligently caused by a vehicle collision. The coverage that provides protection to the

insured from an exposure to the liability is known as the third party coverage.

THE DOCTRINE OF SUBROGATION

This enables the insurer that was paid the loss pursuant of the insured to the property insurance policy to recover the payment from those who belong to the party that was responsible for loss.

Most importantly, the subrogation's principle permits anyone like the insurer who's legally obligated in paying debt to another of the person who owed the payment and enforce the right of the person against the real wrongdoer.

Some policy considerations fall under the doctrine of subrogation. First and foremost, subrogation has the genesis in the indemnity's principle. Even though the insured is entitled to guarantee from the insurer pursuant to the provided coverage under the insurance's policy, the insured will be entitled only to be created whole, not more than it.

Normally, the principles of subrogation prevent the insured from getting a recovery from the insurer under the contractual obligations as well as the 2nd recovery from tortfeasor under the general tort principles. In addition to that, the subrogation rights let the insurer to get payments that were made to the insured who is theoretically must have been created whole throughout those payments.

In conclusion, subrogation advances an essential policy rationale that underlies the tort system through forcing the person who is at fault and has caused the loss to get the burden of acquiring the insurer for the indemnity payments created to its insured as results of the acts as well as omissions of the wrongdoer. This rationale was termed as the tort law's moralistic basis as this has developed in the system.

The latest legal principles have divided the subrogation into 2 fundamental categories, which reflect how the subrogation's right increases. Equitable

subrogation or also referred to as legal subrogation increases when insurers fulfill its obligations to the insured pursuant to the insurance's contract.

THE MADE WHOLE DOCTRINE

This is an equitable defense to reimbursement or subrogation rights of the subrogated insurance carrier or some party that requires before reimbursement or subrogation will be allowed. The insured should be made whole for all of the damages.

In precise words, the meaning of made whole varies from state to state, yet its concept is nonetheless fairly the same in every state.

A well-respected legal treatise defines the made-whole doctrine as follows:

It is widely held that in the absence of contrary statutory law or valid contractual obligation to the contrary, the general rule under the doctrine of equitable subrogation is that whether an insured is entitled to receive recovery for the same loss from more than one source, e.g., the insurer and the tortfeasor, it is only after the insured has been fully compensated for all the loss that the insurer acquires a right to subrogation.

THE DUTIES OF THE INSUANCE COMPANY AFTER A LOSS

The Insurer's Implied Duty to Investigate in Good Faith

This is now mostly recognized in courts in US in which an insurer has the duty to 46 act in good faith and fairly in discharging this contractual responsibilities.

To fulfill this duty, the insurer should investigate the claims of an insured thoroughly and promptly. As the fiduciary, the claims investigation of the insurer should take into consideration the insured's interests and those of insurers.

This was stated by some courts that the insurer's duty is to conduct the claims investigation in good terms is not dependent and unconditional on the performance of the contractual obligations of the insured.

The insurer should not fail or take a position that is groundless to adequately investigate its own position. In addition to that, the duty of the insurer is to investigate the claim of the insured fairly. This should not also be affected by the commencement of the action of the insured against the insurer for breaking the duty with good faith.

The exposure of an insurer to extra-contractual liability as the result of its breach of its duty with fair dealing and good faith may be substantial. This is in accordance to the process of investigation, which must be planned, executed, and monitored carefully to get rid of bad faith claims.

Other Obligations Imposed on Insurers
Majority of states have enacted a legislation that would prohibit insurers from being involved to unfair insurance practices. These are generally defined through the following:

- Misrepresenting insurance policy provisions or pertinent facts regarding to the coverages at an issue;

- Failing to act reasonably and acknowledge promptly upon the communications with respect to the claims arising under the insurance policies;

- Failing to implement and adopt the reasonable standards for the claims' prompt investigation, which increase under the insurance policies;

- Refusing to pay the claims without the need to conduct a reasonable investigation based on the available information;

- Failing to deny or affirm the claims' coverage within the reasonable time after the proof of loss statements were completed;

- Not attempting in good faith to effectuate fair, prompt, and equitable settlements of the claims in which the liability has become clear;

- Compelling the insured to institute the litigation in recovering the amounts because of an insurance policy through offering less than the amounts that were recovered ultimately by those insureds;

- Attempting to settle the claim for less than the amount of which the reasonable man would have believed he was entitled through the reference printed or written advertising material that accompany or made party of the application;

- Attempting to settle the claims on the application's basis, which was altered without the notice to consent or knowledge of the insured;

- Making claims payments to the beneficiaries or insureds not accompanied by the statement that is setting forth the coverage under the payment that were being made;

- Making known to the claimants or insureds the policy of appealing from the arbitration awards in favor of the claimants or insureds for the aim of compelling them in accepting settlements or compromises that are less than the awarded amount in arbitration;

- Delaying the payment of claims or investigation through requiring a claimant, physician or an insured of either in submitting the preliminary claim report as well as requiring the formal proof's subsequent submission of loss forms. Both of these submissions have substantially the similar information;

- Failing to settle the claims promptly where liability became reasonably clear under the portion of an insurance policy coverage to influence the settlement under some portions of an insurance policy coverage;

- Failing to promptly give a reasonable explanation of the insurance policy's basis in relation to the applicable law or facts for denial of the claim for the offer of the compromise settlement.

HOW TO START A DIMINISHED VALUE CLAIM

Will You Need Help in Settling Your Diminished Value Claim?

The answer is big YES. The car insurance industry always comes up with new excuses just for them to not pay what they owe on the Diminished Value claims. To the uninitiated, several arguments actually make sense. However, for trained professionals, many heard all arguments before and they know how to deal with one of them.

Over the past several years, the group of diminished value appraisers has mushroomed. At present, there are discount diminished value appraisers who will pick your pocket to whatever they can acquire in exchange for the useless reports that do not have value. The industry of insurance even seems to be underwriting several late entries in an effort to reduce their payments on diminished value claims.

Can You Collect Diminished Value Through State-by-State?

From the insurance company of the party that is at fault, it is very possible to get Diminished Value. Well, you can collect to each state except Michigan.

If the party that is at fault has no insurance, you can still collect diminished value. This can be done under Uninsured Motorist Coverage of your own policy, but this is only possible in some states including California, Arkansas, Alaska, District of Columbia, Delaware, Hawaii, Georgia, Illinois, Georgia, Louisiana, Indiana, Mississippi, Maryland, New Mexico, New Jersey, Ohio, North Carolina, Oregon, South Carolina, Rhode Island, Texas, Tennessee, Utah, Virginia, Vermont, West Virginia, and Washington.

From the Collision Coverage of Your Own Policy, you can also collect Diminished value most particularly in Kansas or Georgia. However, Kansas

may subject to some policy limitations. You can also get if you are from Washington.

The 17c Formula

On the 28th of November 2001, the Georgia Supreme Court has issued a ruling in the case of the State Farm Mutual Automobile Insurance Company v. Mabry. This court ruling has stated that the physical damage that may result from the covered event may reduce the vehicle's value even if the repairs returned it to its pre-loss condition.

The court also determined that the involved insurance company in the case is obliged to assess the diminution of value together with the physical damage's elements when the policy holder make the general claim of loss.

The Mabry case is a class action lawsuit that involves more than twenty five thousand insurance claims. To compensate claimants under the lawsuit, the court has agreed to the generic formula's temporary use.

It's not difficult to understand why a formula was utilized in this case. It is because of huge number of vehicles that are involved and the difficulty in having a real appraiser who assesses the post-wreck amount and market value in comparison to the pre-accident value.

Since the year 2001, State Farm as well as some insurance companies have been using the 17c formula as well as citing precedent. Their logic is basically flawed. Unless, you took part of the class, this ruling may not be applied to you.

Moreover, the Georgia Insurance commissioner who has executed a directive that instructs insurance companies not to consider language in their correspondence that states the 17c is the final or legal determination

of Diminished Value. Also, the directive stated that insurers are needed to consider the evidence from the consumers that are referencing the loss in value.

The commissioner has also continued to say that the GA insurance doesn't endorse 17c. This is due to the negative publicity 17c receives. Some insurance companies like USAA for instance use 17c yet they call this something else like Diminished Value worksheet or Georgia worksheet. Regardless, if the method utilizes the similar components as the 17c

State Laws On Diminished Value

Georgia Claim Info
Georgia Statute Of Limitations: 4 Years
Uninsured Motorist CoverageYES
Available For At Fault Party: YES

Alabama Claim Info
Alabama Statute Of Limitations: 6 Years
Uninsured Motorist Coverage: NO
Available For At Fault Party: NO

Florida Claim Info
Florida Statute Of Limitations: 4 Years
Uninsured Motorist Coverage: NO
Available For At Fault Party: NO

South Carolina Claim Info
SC Statute Of Limitations: 3 Years
Uninsured Motorist Coverage: Yes
Available For At Fault Party: NO

Tennessee Claim Info
Tennessee Statute Of Limitations: 3 Years
Uninsured Motorist Coverage: Yes
Available For At Fault Party: NO

Mississippi Claim Info
Mississippi Statute Of Limitations: CALL
Uninsured Motorist Coverage: Yes
Available For At Fault Party: NO

Louisiana Claim Info
Louisiana Statute Of Limitations: 1 Year
Uninsured Motorist Coverage: Yes
Available For At Fault Party: NO

Texas Claim Info
Texas Statute Of Limitations: 2 Years
Uninsured Motorist Coverage: Yes
Available For At Fault Party: NO

Arkansas Claim Info
Arkansas Statute Of Limitations: 3 Years
Uninsured Motorist Coverage: Yes
Available For At Fault Party: NO

North Carolina Claim Info
North Carolina Statute Of Limitations: 3 Years
Uninsured Motorist Coverage: Yes
Available For At Fault Party: NO

Oklahoma Claim Info
Oklahoma Statute Of Limitations: 2 Years
Uninsured Motorist Coverage: NO
Available For At Fault Party: NO

New Mexico Claim Info
New Mexico Statute Of Limitations: 4 Years
Uninsured Motorist Coverage: Yes
Available For At Fault Party: NO

Arizona Claim Info
Arizona Statute Of Limitations: 2 Years
Uninsured Motorist Coverage: NO
Available For At Fault Party: NO

Virginia Claim Info
Virginia Statute Of Limitations: 5 Years
Uninsured Motorist Coverage: Yes
Available For At Fault Party: NO

West Virginia Claim Info
West Virginia Statute Of Limitations: 2 Years
Uninsured Motorist Coverage: Yes
Available For At Fault Party: NO

Kentucky Claim Info
Kentucky Statute Of Limitations: 5 Years
Uninsured Motorist Coverage: NO
Available For At Fault Party: NO

Missouri Claim Info
Missouri Statute Of Limitations: 5 Years
Uninsured Motorist Coverage: NO
Available For At Fault Party: NO

Kansas Claim Info
Kansas Statute Of Limitations: 2 Years
Uninsured Motorist Coverage: NO
Available For At Fault Party: NO

Colorado Claim Info
Colorado Statute Of Limitations: 2 Years
Uninsured Motorist Coverage
Available For At Fault Party: NO

Utah Claim Info
Utah Statute Of Limitations: 3 Years
Uninsured Motorist Coverage: Yes
Available For At Fault Party: NO

Nevada Claim Info
Nevada Statute Of Limitations: 3 Years
Uninsured Motorist Coverage: NO
Available For At Fault Party: NO

California Claim Info
California Statute Of Limitations: 3 Years
Uninsured Motorist Coverage: Yes
Available For At Fault Party: NO

Oregon Claim Info
Oregon Statute Of Limitations: 6 Years
Uninsured Motorist Coverage: Yes
Available For At Fault Party: NO

Washington Claim Info
Washington Statute Of Limitations: 3 Years
Uninsured Motorist Coverage: Yes
Available For At Fault Party: NO

Idaho Claim Info
Idaho Statute Of Limitations: 3 Years
Uninsured Motorist Coverage: NO
Available For At Fault Party: NO

Montana Claim Info
Montana Statute Of Limitations: 2 Years
Uninsured Motorist Coverage: NO
Available For At Fault Party: NO

Wyoming Claim Info
Wyoming Statute Of Limitations: 4 Years
Uninsured Motorist Coverage: NO
Available For At Fault Party: NO

Nebraska Claim Info
Nebraska Statute Of Limitations: 4 Years
Uninsured Motorist Coverage: NO
Available For At Fault Party: NO

South Dakota Claim Info
South Dakota Statute Of Limitations: 6 Years
Uninsured Motorist Coverage: NO
Available For At Fault Party: NO

North Dakota Claim Info
North Dakota Statute Of Limitations: 6
Uninsured Motorist Coverage: NO
Available For At Fault Party: NO

Minnesota Claim Info
Minnesota Statute Of Limitations: 6 Years
Uninsured Motorist Coverage: NO
Available For At Fault Party: NO

Iowa Claim Info
Iowa Statute Of Limitations: 2 Years
Uninsured Motorist Coverage
Available For At Fault Party: NO

Wisconsin Claim Info
Wisconsin Statute Of Limitations: 6 Years
Uninsured Motorist Coverage: NO
Available For At Fault Party: NO

Illinois Claim Info
Illinois Statute Of Limitations: 5 Years
Uninsured Motorist Coverage: Yes
Available For At Fault Party: NO

Indiana Claim Info
Indiana Statute Of Limitations: 6 Years
Uninsured Motorist Coverage: Yes
Available For At Fault Party: NO

Michigan Claim Info
Michigan Statute Of Limitations: 3 Years
Uninsured Motorist Coverage: NO
Available For At Fault Party: NO

Ohio Claim Info
Ohio Statute Of Limitations: 4 Years
Uninsured Motorist Coverage: Yes
Available For At Fault Party: NO

Pennsylvania Claim Info
Pennsylvania Statute Of Limitations: 2 Years
Uninsured Motorist Coverage: NO
Available For At Fault Party: NO

Maryland Claim Info
Maryland Statute Of Limitations: 3 Years
Uninsured Motorist Coverage: Yes
Available For At Fault Party: NO

New Jersey Claim Info
New Jersey Statute Of Limitations: 6 Years
Uninsured Motorist Coverage: Yes
Available For At Fault Party: NO

Delaware Claim Info
Delaware Statute Of Limitations: 2 Years
Uninsured Motorist Coverage: Yes
Available For At Fault Party: NO

New York Claim Info
New York Statute Of Limitations: 3 Years
Uninsured Motorist Coverage: NO
Available For At Fault Party: NO

Connecticut Claim Info
Connecticut Statute Of Limitations: 2 Years
Uninsured Motorist Coverage: NO
Available For At Fault Party: NO

Rhode Island Claim Info
Rhode Island Statute Of Limitations: 10 Years
Uninsured Motorist Coverage: Yes
Available For At Fault Party: NO

Massachusetts Claim Info
Massachusetts Statute Of Limitations: 3 Years
Uninsured Motorist Coverage: NO
Available For At Fault Party: NO

New Hampshire Claim Info
New Hampshire Statute Of Limitations: 3 Years
Uninsured Motorist Coverage: NO
Available For At Fault Party: NO

Vermont Claim Info
Vermont Statute Of Limitations: 3 Years
Uninsured Motorist Coverage: Yes
Available For At Fault Party: NO

Maine Claim Info
Maine Statute Of Limitations: 6 Years
Uninsured Motorist Coverage: NO
Available For At Fault Party: NO

DISCLAIMER

This book is for informational purposes only: It does not provide business or legal advise, and should not be relied on as such. Neither the author nor the publisher guarantees or warrants that the information in this book is accurate, complete, up to date, or will produce certain financial results.

www.ingramcontent.com/pod-product-compliance
Lightning Source LLC
Chambersburg PA
CBHW071600170526
45166CB00004B/1736